LOVE

JOHNS HOPKINS
UNIVERSITY PRESS

AARHUS UNIVERSITY PRESS

Love

ANNE MARIE PAHUUS

LOVE

© Anne Marie Pahuus
and Johns Hopkins University Press 2025
Layout and cover: Camilla Jørgensen, Trefold
Cover photograph: Poul Ib Henriksen
Publishing editor: Karina Bell Ottosen
Translated from the Danish by Heidi Flegal
Printed by Narayana Press, Denmark
Printed in Denmark 2025

ISBN 978-1-4214-4785-8 (pbk)
ISBN 978-1-4214-4786-5 (ebook)

Library of Congress Control Number: 2023942078

*Special discounts are available for bulk purchases of this
book. For more information, please contact Special Sales at
specialsales@jh.edu.*

Published in the United States by:

Johns Hopkins University Press
2715 North Charles Street
Baltimore, MD 21218
www.press.jhu.edu

Published with the generous support of the
Aarhus University Research Foundation

Purchase in Denmark: ISBN 978-87-7597-522-8

Aarhus University Press
Helsingforsgade 25
8200 Aarhus N
Denmark
www.aarhusuniversitypress.dk

PEER
REVIEWED

MIX
Paper
FSC FSC® C010651

CONTENTS

WHAT IS LOVE?

A BIG WORD

Love is a big word, yet it slips so easily from our lips. In all cultures we have poems about having our hearts broken, torn apart or even stolen away when we are abandoned. But we also use the word "love" to describe much less radical emotional experiences. This grand word is not reserved only for the greatest emotions and the most decisive actions in life. Love is also an everyday thing, virtually woven into the fabric of our daily activities. On the way to and from school or work, at the bus stop, on our morning run – everywhere we listen to songs about love, especially unrequited love.

Love reaches into every corner of our lives. It is the spark in our most memorable moments, and it is the daily glue in our lives with children, spouses and lovers. But it is also the constant flow of words and images that accumulate into one of the most overworked motifs in the films, series, books, podcasts and music of our culture's entertainment industry: romantic love.

So what is love, actually? Put simply, it is the intimate relationships we have with other people. Relationships so emotionally intense they can shape our will and our desires.

In erotic love this intimacy is tangibly manifested in

bodily contact of a sexual nature. Here the intensity is associated with physical desire, but affectionate lovers also share devotion, trust and a sense of belonging. Non-sexual intimacy can be just as sweeping and powerful. Just look at parents and children. Even adult children are encompassed by their parents' tenderness, pride, trust and wish to protect them. We have similar relationships with our closest friends when love, friendship and respect blend into one, as in the Greek word *philia*, which translations of ancient texts render as both "friendship" and as "love".

In other words, love is made up of emotions – intense and in the plural. At its core, love is a mixture of various warm feelings fuelled by our desire to be with another person. But warm feelings are not always pleasant, and they span emotions that range from happiness to sorrow. Taking a cue from the British singer-songwriter Bryan Ferry, you might say we are all "slaves to love", for better and for worse. It hurts to miss a loved one, or to struggle with doubt and distrust. Even when not pathological or obsessive, jealousy can still be an agonizing, debilitating force.

LOVE IS INSIDE US

Theoretically, a person's inner self can be divided into three parts that enable us to think, to decide and to feel. The first is cool and well-reasoned. The second is bold and inclined to act, and the third is hot and emotional. Love is forged by our heat and our will to act. Blind passion combined with brave choices.

We are directly motivated by what we love, whether seeking to protect it from external threats or overcoming obstacles and separation. The most intense of aggression, regardless of gender, surfaces when parents are prepared to resort to extreme measures to protect their child. The greatest hardship and torment we endure is suffered while hoping to be reunited with a loved one. In essence, love frames our lives and actions, shaping our plans and goals. Love is everywhere, although it cannot explain everything, and it informs and influences the choices we make – more or less consciously – to embrace or reject, include or ignore.

Less conscious choices are often made when we react to love. A case in point was a young female patient of the Swiss psychoanalyst Ludwig Binswanger. She had become mute after her mother refused to let her meet with her beloved, a young officer in the navy. At the time, psychoanalysts were generally obliged not to interfere with the personal lives of their patients, but in this case Binswanger made an exception. He admitted the young woman for treatment in 1929. Wracked by bouts of convulsive hiccuping and hyperventilation, she had suddenly lost the power of speech. When he learned her seizures had begun after she was forbidden to see the man she was in love with, Binswanger chose to treat her silence as an unconscious decision to stop communicating with the world around her. Fortunately, her hiccuping and mutism were cured after Binswanger convinced her mother to let the young couple give their love a chance. Although physical, the young woman's symptoms expressed something mental: an unconscious choice not to "swallow" – accept – her mother's decision. During her seizures Binswanger performed very concrete interventions on her neck and throat, helping her to swallow. This also helped the mother to see the futility in forcing her daughter to choose between one kind of love (her mother) and another (a man). Incidentally, the young woman's love for the officer did not last, but she did not suffer a relapse of her condition, since the pressure of choosing had been removed.

A BALANCED SOUL

The division of a person into three parts can be traced back to ancient Greek philosophy, particularly in the works of Plato. He described love as both an internal and an external force, linking a person's inner qualities – such as reason, will and emotion – with their actions and pursuits in the world. He saw love as a driving force that connects our inner selves with our external efforts and endeavors. Plato argued that just as love requires the harmony of the three parts of a person – reason, will and emotion – so too must people work together to create an ideal state. In his vision of this state, society is organized into distinct classes representing reason, courage and appetite. Only by achieving a just state and a balanced soul can humanity reach the highest truth, the greatest good and eternal beauty. For Plato, human happiness mirrors this ideal. It is a union of three elements: truth as the ideal of reason, goodness as the ideal of will, and beauty as the ideal of emotion. We will look more closely at this last element, beauty, in one of Plato's dialogues, his favorite format for philosophical writing. *Symposium*, "the drinking party", is one of Western culture's most important texts on the nature of love, specifically the type of love Plato refers to as eros (which, capitalised, denotes the Greek deity of love).

Like Plato did in ancient times, we too must approach love in its full scope, prepared to explore beyond mere feelings and understand its broader implications. Today we still see love as reaching beyond emotional attachments and love stories, moving into the field of what is good or morally beneficial, just as Plato pointed out. The fact is, love is much more than a personal emotion or a central theme in art and entertainment. It also encompasses our significant relationships with others. This makes love a force not only in forming bonds between people but also in making communication possible, and in allowing community, trust and acceptance to arise. Love not only shapes our experience of happiness but also defines our responsibilities.

YOU'RE RESPONSIBLE FOR YOUR ROSE

We often say love works in mysterious ways, not always comprehending why people choose one partner over another. But whether, in choosing, we commit ourselves body and soul or only touch each other's lives briefly, such meetings bring consequences and responsibilities. Emotional involvement and love-driven connections are always ethically relevant.

Consider a teenager uncertain of how to prioritise friends, school, work and sports activities. Not just anyone can step in with support. Parents are obligated and must guide and understand in ways no one else can. Not because parents necessarily know their child best, but because they are the ones who love their child most. The people who love a child are the people the child dares to lean on, be dependent upon. Love is reciprocated with trust and affection, which in turn lays the mind open to happiness and vulnerability.

For couples, love also means daring to meet trust with trust. Daring to love and be loved. Trusting we will not be rejected when revealing our mind to the other. Love makes us responsible for those to whom we bind ourselves with ties of love, and who rely on our devotion and our care. As the philosophical fox explains in *The Little Prince*, a whimsical tale by the French author Antoine de Saint-Exupéry published during World War II: "You become responsible forever for what you've tamed. You're responsible for your rose."

SEEING WITH THE HEART

Love is an important part of lived human life. This makes it a precious element in our lives we can either nurture or neglect. It takes repeated, wilful acts to benefit the object of our love. As many couples realise after spending several years together, it takes work to make love work, and our labours of love give sustenance to the choice we originally made with our heart.

The point is that in love we see and understand with our hearts. By seating love in the heart rather than the brain, we illustrate that loving can be well-founded even though our reasoning may seem baffling. More precisely, we stop reasoning before we've even begun. We stop, convinced that the reason is our beloved. We didn't specifically choose him because he is tall, kind-hearted, smart, or organised, and that's not why we stay with him. Then again, had he not been smart and kind, we might not have noticed him in the first place. The qualities of a beloved partner contribute to the image we form of them.

If someone asks us to, we can easily explain things like how well our partner's practical, sensible approach to life complements our own dreamier disposition. But when it comes to love, that's not what counts. It's not his IQ or his talent as an organiser that makes me willing to do anything for him. What counts is who he is.

The French polymath Blaise Pascal already clarified this several centuries ago in the *Pensées*, a note-based volume of his thoughts published posthumously in 1670. Here, playing on the word *raison*, he famously phrases how choices of the heart have their own impenetrable reasoning. Like its English sister, the French word *raison* expresses both "cause" and "intellect". Hence his famous quote: "The heart has its reasons which reason knows nothing of."

The inscrutability of love does not mean love is limited to an inner realm inaccessible to others. Even so, what typifies the choices we make on behalf of love is that we put ourselves at risk, at stake – we give ourselves over to someone else. The act of surrender itself embodies a desire that can surprise both ourselves and others.

Such desire is often asymmetrical. Love is not always returned in kind. Some give themselves over in a way the other person cannot reciprocate. We must sometimes ignore an appeal for mutual surrender if it is awkward, inconvenient, emotionally draining. Yes, we may be failing to appreciate a valuable thing, but had we embarked on a relationship without the warm feelings that requires, we would be making a personal sacrifice that was not in the best interest of the other. Acting out of pity or for the sake of convenience makes both parties unfree.

With all this in mind, initially it is fair to define love as warm feelings that are cultivated through a certain amount of wilful exertion. We can also acknowledge that giving ourselves over to another person creates powerful ties that bind our choices and our will to that other person, making us responsible for them. Finally, we can establish that love can be mutual and reciprocal, although that is not always the case.

THE ESSENCE OF LOVE

MOVED TO TEARS

In love, everything is possible except indifference. Pity can be mistaken for love, and love can even turn to hate, but being superficial towards a loved one is incredibly hard. Does this mean love is always solemn and soulful? Certainly not. Often love is brief and light-hearted. Many paintings and narratives depict love in ways that stir our emotions at a seemingly superficial level, but it is important to remember that such perceived triviality does not stem from the feelings themselves. Love may seem clichéd not because the feelings are flawed, but because it is often portrayed in ways that lack depth, reducing it to shallow sentimentality. Emotions cannot lie, but they can be cultivated for their own sake, and words can inflate them till they become worthless. Our feelings can get lost in waves of clever dialogue, which often overshadow our direct experience of love. This is why film is such a powerful medium for depicting wordless moments like a kiss or embrace. Such scenes can convey a deep sense of a relationship's spirit. Whether the famous depiction of Kate Winslet and Leonardo DiCaprio on the prow of the *Titanic* represents love as exemplary or clichéd is left to the interpretation of the viewer.

When we cultivate love and attempt to capture its

essence, we often find ourselves drawn towards the banal rather than the intellectual. We can be moved to tears even by mediocre imagery. Paintings of teary-eyed Romani children, for instance, clichéd as they may be, evoke a profound sense of helplessness riggering memories of our own childhood – of feeling lost and alone. Such vague feelings of loss and consolation make us teary-eyed ourselves in response to kitsch. While our original emotions may be genuine, art can sometimes exploit them to elicit a certain reaction rather than exploring the actual reasons behind the emotion being expressed, be it desolation or hope, joy or sorrow. If a romantic plot is too simplistic, the love it portrays often seems equally dull.

So would we be better off simply leaving the theme of love alone? By constantly flogging the topic, do we not risk reducing it to something stale, unoriginal? Or risk theoretically intellectualising that which ought to be lived instead? And am I, as an author, even doing philosophy a service by dealing with love as a philosophical theme? Some philosophers gladly let the psychologists deal with issues of human emotion. Others, meanwhile, choose to deal with love but remain aware of the dangers of over-intellectualisation. The Danish thinker and theologian Søren Kierkegaard belongs to the latter group: those who have dealt with love in detail while being careful not to see love as one specific thing. Someone who really loves, he says, can hardly derive any joy, satisfaction or progress from trying to puzzle out a definition.

Perhaps this means we ought to curb our interest in

analysing intimate, loving relationships and simply leave love, mental and physical, to those who feel it. How deeply should we delve? Instead we could apply ourselves to other, wider theoretical issues. Why not Nature, or the societies humans are able to create? How much should we emphasise the intimate?

THE GREATEST OF THESE IS LOVE

Only recently, relatively speaking, did love become a personal matter between mothers and fathers, parents and children. Before the nineteenth century, no clear division existed between, for example, the laws of Nature and the freedom of the people on the one hand and love on the other. Until then several philosophers, including Plato in antiquity and the Dutch philosopher Baruch de Spinoza in the 1600s, understood love as a glimpse into the necessities of the Universe, into the Divine. Rumi, a Sufi mystic and poet of the 1200s, held that without love the world would be frozen and lifeless. "Know", he wrote, "that the wheeling heavens are turned by the waves of Love."

The apostle Paul probably presented the best-known Christian interpretation of love – "charity" in the scripture – as the centre of all things in a letter to the congregation at Corinth: "Love is patient, love is kind. It does not envy, it does not boast, it is not proud. It does not dishonor others, it is not self-seeking, it is not easily angered, it keeps no record of wrongs. Love does not delight in evil but rejoices with the truth. It always protects, always trusts, always hopes, always perseveres".

Paul sees faith and hope as two of the three preconditions for everything else, concluding that "now these three remain: faith, hope and love. But the greatest of these is love."

Love is still the biggest thing around, but God and the Universe no longer define the boundaries between daily living and the parts of our lives governed by love. Today love's main function is to create and maintain the sort of interpersonal relationships that challenge our firm belief in the individual's right to self-determination. In short: Love makes us see another person as more important to our lives than we are. This can be an overwhelming experience, but once we have come through it we are changed forever. In this sense love reaches beyond close personal relations and sets the stage for all manner of trust, acceptance and respect. When we can give ourselves to another person and spend the rest of our lives with them, then, as the American poet Walt Whitman says in "Song of the Open Road", we are laying the foundation for an entire society:

Mon enfant! I give you my hand!
I give you my love, more precious than money,
I give you myself, before preaching or law;
Will you give me your self?
Will you come travel with me?
Shall we stick by each other as long as we live?

THE RECIPROCITY OF LOVE

Love creates lasting reciprocity. It takes love to even make a person capable of reciprocating trust with trust. Love can also be institutionalised in a contract of marriage, a couple's promise meant to last "until death do us part".

Over the past 200 years we have become increasingly preoccupied with romantic love and the feelings it evokes. In the 1950s the Danish writer Karen Blixen offered a critique of this shift that remains relevant today. Blixen saw great value in the way marriage, tied to lineage, heritage, and even the pursuit of greatness in life, alleviated the emotional burden placed on love. In post-feudal societies, societal functions became separated from family and marital connections. For Blixen, marriage was not supposed to be driven solely by personal feelings or transient emotions. Instead, she held, it ought to be anchored in a deeper sense of value – one that connects individuals to their heritage, their familial legacy, and a broader sense of life's meaning. This perspective provided marriage with a depth and stability that the modern focus on romantic love often lacks.

It was artists, poets and painters of the Romantic age who propagated the idea of great love, linking it to the idea of finding and marrying a "one and only true love". In Blixen's opinion, this was detrimental to marriage and to love.

Several decades later another well-known Danish author, Suzanne Brøgger, echoed Blixen in this view. In her 1973 debut *Deliver Us from Love*, Brøgger exposed the emptiness behind the "declarations of happiness", where people publicly boast about their perfect marriages. They broadcast their joy and bliss, with the celebrity press hailing every couple as "a match made in heaven" – until the divorce announcement is made.

The concept of true love as an ideal certainly spread with the Romantics, but its legacy goes back to the chivalrous poetry and courtly love of the Middle Ages. A prime example is the legend of Tristan and Isolde. In this tale, as in many chivalric stories, true love is depicted as a powerful force, a blind passion that surmounts all obstacles. Tristan was betrothed to another woman, Iseult of the White Hands, but he fell in love with Isolde, an Irish princess promised to King Mark of Cornwall, and she fell in love with him. The two met in secret and continued their affair in various hidden locations – the castle garden, the forest, and even Isolde's wedding bed while her husband was away. We see their love intensified by the adversity they face, which both challenges and strengthens their bond.

Such intense passion is "unsuitable for cohabitation" according to Swiss cultural theorist Denis de Rougemont in his 1939 study *Love in the Western World*. He describes this form of love in Western culture as *Liebestod*: love that is willing to die for, or more precisely, love that can only be fully realised in death. This is exemplified by Tristan and Isolde, who, after their tragic deaths, are buried in a chapel, one on either side of the chancel. From Tristan's grave, a rosebush grows across to reach Isolde's.

It was this concept of passion that Romantic thinking internalised and remade as a spiritual ideal. From 1750 onwards, literary characters hung suspended between passions incompatible with lived lives of cohabitation and marriages emptied of all content but love. Perhaps this dilemma still haunts us today. Could that be one reason why so many people give up on marriage? Daily life stepping in where we expect ardent, true love, dreaming of some testing, forbidden passion that defies marriage altogether?

That may be the case, but marriage still frequently scaffolds our physical love and the children we bear, although pregnancy and child-rearing no longer require a marital framework. Singles now have children openly, whereas the pre-1950s era had no effective contraception, widely confining sex and conception to marriage. One particular aim of this was to protect (and guard) women and children. Today, all that has changed, but even before 1950 the main content of marriage was not protection. It was, and still is, love. Whether formalised or not, stable partnerships still frame love for over half of adults in most countries. The rest live as singles, with or without partners or lovers.

COSMOS NO MORE

Within marriages and outside them, modern people are left more to their own devices in their search for love than people in antiquity or in feudal societies. Back then, order reigned. Antiquity had *kosmos*, a given order where gods and demigods relegated humans to their proper place. This concept is what enabled Plato to write that "human nature will not easily find a helper better than love". The Bible also pays tribute to divine order in the apostle Paul's words:

"Now I know in part; then I shall know fully, even as I have been fully known [...] and the greatest of these is love".

Even today our cultural heritage tells us love comes to us from outside ourselves. In other words, we still expect Mr. Right to turn up on our doorstep, but we do not have love placed in a well-ordered system, as Plato did, complete with ideas of the Seventh Heaven and the demigod or "daimon" Eros to help us decode them. There is no longer a direct link between what we see in another person and the great cosmos of which that person, every person, is a part.

That's why it is harder for us than it was for Plato to say we adore the whole world when adoring the beauty we see in one person. We no longer look into the all-embracing Universe when we look into the eyes of our beloved and surrender to love. Our universe is too cluttered with contradicting explanations of everything under the sun: natural evolution, the environment, market forces, human health and illness in mind and body. Things are no longer allotted their own little slot in the cosmos where they fit snugly – aided by Eros or by God. Our expectations of harmony and order, however, remain intact. This may lie at the root of the modern conundrum of wishing, in our own lives, that love can be all, do all, conquer all, even as we've lost our sense of a greater whole. What remains is for us to test our way forward, putting one foot in front of the other, even though our ultimate goal is lost from sight.

WHO CAN EXPLAIN LOVE?

Poets and philosophers are not alone in exploring the

essence of love; scientists also find the topic increasingly fascinating. However, their hypotheses and conclusions are often seen as definitive answers, which can be misleading, so it is important to remain cautious and critical of any single explanation.

Psychology, for instance, believes we choose partners based on patterns of attachment formed in infancy. However, if this alone could explain the essence of love, then psychology would be reducing adult love to the mental equivalent of a cubbyhole where we retreat to lick the wounds of our childhood.

Biology alone cannot provide a conclusive explanation of love choices, but it can shed light on certain factors. For example, it can explain the role of non-scented, nasally registered pheromones emitted by potential mates nearby. However, focusing solely on these biological aspects overlooks the cultural and social patterns that psychology identifies as crucial.

Sociology helps us to understand when and how social upheaval and crisis can stimulate amorous feelings, and to recognise links between personal break-ups and social revolutions. Likewise, economics can look at equality, income growth and education levels to calculate a given marriage's probability of success – and so on and so forth. All interesting factors, but inconclusive.

I'M YOUR MAN

The Canadian singer-songwriter Leonard Cohen is performing at Rosenborg Castle's park in the heart of

Copenhagen. A Danish newspaper journalist in the crowd senses the love flowing from the audience towards the stage. A 27-year-old female fan tells the journalist, "He's the second man in my life." She is at the concert with her husband, who introduced her to Cohen's music. But how can Cohen be "a man in her life", despite his numerous recordings and performances? Are her feelings for Cohen and her love for her husband comparable? Are her feelings for Cohen really a form of love? Like many fans, she may feel that Cohen is speaking directly to her, singing out his adoration, willing to do anything to be with his beloved – wear a mask, step into a boxing ring, walk across the sand, anything. Always at the ready, his unfailing response is "I'm your man".

Poems and lyrics like Cohen's are often brimming with love, but they can also bring deep sadness. Even though a scar only happens when the word is made flesh, to paraphrase an evocative expression from his first novel, *My Favorite Game*, poetically phrased love is a real part of the love that is felt. It is not poetry separated from emotions. For one thing, thinking brings emotional clarification. For another, we often remember written words better than our own more randomly assembled words. In former times snippets of hymns would sneak into our language, and we would all need our hankies for "Here Comes the Bride". In recent decades lines from popular songs have had us envisioning a stay at "Heartbreak Hotel" or reminiscing how "Nothing Compares 2 U".

We recognise ourselves, we feel addressed, and we

empathise with the people whose emotions are expressed by fictitious first-person narrators. Pity, if not always compassion, for the long-suffering protagonist is also an important instrument in art. It is heart-wrenching to follow the fate of ill-starred couples like Othello and Desdemona, Catherine and Heathcliffe; to see love founder in *Brokeback Mountain* or *The English Patient*.

So love, with its heroines and heroes, aids and adversaries, makes for good stories and we, the audience, willingly add on and identify with characters we know only from the narrative. The great German author Johann Wolfgang von Goethe wrote *The Sorrows of Young Werther*, chronicling a young man's torments at being unable to wed his beloved Charlotte, ending in his suicide to find release. A key work in the *Sturm und Drang* movement, the German original appeared in 1774 and made an indelible impression on generations of readers. Reactions in the 1770s included a Danish ban on the book, issued by the church and the faculty of theology in Copenhagen to prevent the numerous real-life suicides ostensibly motivated by the book's romanticised account of death.

Identifying with fictional characters, whether out of empathy or concern about ending up like them, can broaden our understanding of gender identity. People of all genders recognise that gender encompasses a wide range of appearances, behaviours, and expressions. Fictional characters show us various ways to embody different genders, and we also relate to real people who may or may not share our gender.

The key is that individuals use their gender in diverse ways. In the workplace, for instance, we may use gestures, comments, and clothing to highlight or downplay our gender identity. This is true in many social contexts, including cafés, clubs, private dinners, and family gatherings, each with its own unwritten rules for gendered interactions.

Our understanding of gender is influenced by how we see others represent themselves and by how we are guided in understanding our own bodies. Even early and awkward romantic experiences contribute to shaping our sense of gender identity.

Awkward or not, the proverbial "first time" is often an overwhelming experience that can make us feel more hesitant than resolved. A short story by the Danish writer Dan Turèll describes the initial-encounter, first-impression situation as a recurring thing. His narrator begins, 13 times over, with "The first time I met her". As his account progresses, we realise he is talking about his "first times" – with 13 different girls, each one unique. One girl at the back of the classroom, a blue-eyed blonde, catches his eye after the summer holidays. Another girl, dark-skinned and radiant, he spots at a concert, unfortunately with another man. A third girl and our narrator hang about at a party after everyone else has left. A fourth rants and raves at him, then seduces him, and the list goes on.

I LOVE ...

Love is much more than gender-based interaction. It is also the intense emotional bond that arises when eye contact is established between an infant and its parent. However, beyond erotic experiences and parental love we also use the words "I love" about lots of other things that are very down to earth.

We love ice cream and trips to the seashore, but emotional attachment to this cold, creamy substance is hardly what we feel when exclaiming we'd "love an ice cream" on a hot summer's day after cycling to the beach. So why use this word about a dollop of ice-cold food served in a conical wafer? Why apply the same phrase to the greatest and the smallest things in life: a professional musician, a cold treat, and the love of our life?

We may use language carelessly but the word is still the same, so there must be some perceived link between, say, certain foodstuffs and powerful bonds between people. The experience of enjoying a frozen dairy product with someone we care for embodies a pleasure we attempt to convey using a word for positive emotions. Plus, of course, the simple joy of taste and texture, that sweet melting on the tongue that makes ice cream such a favourite.

Mostly it's when we are least concerned with fathoming what the emotion really covers, or what sensations gave rise to it, that we find ourselves blurting out that we "love this" or "love doing that". We could easily describe this more accurately, grade the experience on a scale of enjoyment, actively think about the value of the thing, or just make a linguistic effort. When life becomes more serious, fraught with illness, grief or separation, we may begin to think more consciously about the words we choose to discern between who or what we love and the things we quite like but can easily do without.

"I love" in metaphorical and colloquial language is probably so frequent because we usually feel no need to distinguish between comfort, pleasure and love. All we really want to do is acknowledge the value of the things or people we care about.

THE PATTERNS OF LOVE

"Being in love," or infatuation, may last a year at most, while "loving" can last a lifetime. To move beyond the initial stages of infatuation, we need to understand the patterns of attachment we carry from early childhood, which are shaped by our relationships with primary caregivers.

Psychology generally employs three different types of attachment. Children who feel securely attached to their mother early on in life will find it easy to trust a partner later. Some children grow up with a mother who was not always present, and they tend to develop nervous or anxious feelings that make them prone to insecurity and jealousy. Other children have a distant or non-existent relationship with their mother, and they react by expecting relationships to be the same, often seeking in adulthood to make their way alone.

As the short-lived "in love" phase indicates, few of the numerous people we fall for come to play a significant role in our lives. However, the primary identity-creating bonds between parents and children make a lasting imprint on our love lives.

We are tied to our parents. Part of our identity is linked to them. There is an emotional bond. For a child, this is what invariably makes the absence of a parent difficult, causing them to question who they are as a person. Later on, many experience the child–parent bond from the adult perspective when they have children of their own. "Attachment" is a pale, dry term for that bond. In parenthood many perceive, for the first time, something beyond themselves that is unconditionally more important than they are.

Love makes us think about the world and discover unknown value in it. As human beings we cannot help but attribute value to the world, because the world contains the potential and the predisposition to love. We therefore connect with people and things in the world, and we come to care about how others feel. The tasks, situations and roles that are part of being someone on whom others depend, to whom others are bound, become crucial. In other words, love engenders happiness and trust in life, on a par with the basic moods allowing us to recognise death as part of the human condition. According to existential thinkers like the Danish theologian K.E. Løgstrup or the German-American philosopher Hannah Arendt, who both explored the role of love and respect in human life, joy is as essential as anxiety. Unlike thinkers such as Sartre, who focus on angst, Løgstrup and Arendt emphasise joy's grounding role in relationships as central to human existence.

FALLING IN LOVE – INTO THE VOID

Sigmund Freud, the founder of psychoanalysis, has
thoroughly described infantile sexuality and its significance
to adult life, and by extension to the love lives of adults. His
thinking has been widely misconstrued – since his point is
not that children's sexuality corresponds to that of adults.
Not at all. He simply says that the child's developmental
phases associated with the oral, anal and genital regions are
decisive to their psychosexual development, with pleasure
and pain as driving forces. Why can we find sweet romantic
stories *and* grisly crime stories entertaining? Because we
find even unpleasurable emotions or "affects" compelling,
sometimes actively seeking out affects such as fear, shock
and revulsion.

The affect felt in adult love can be so ecstatic that,
according to the American psychoanalyst Rollo May, it feels
like falling into a void – giving away one's inner self without
knowing whether it will ever be returned. In this sense May
likens certain aspects of being in love with the rapture of a
mystic communing with God. On the connection between
death and love, he explains that those who haven't already
realised how strong that link is find out when they have a
child. The vulnerability is tangible in a parent's affection
for their baby, however robust the child may be. The fear
of losing a child is the greatest fear of all, and such loss can
make it almost impossible to go on living.

OPPOSITES ATTRACT

There are many emotions associated with love, but are

they the same for everyone? For instance, do people of different genders or backgrounds feel the same when they love someone, or make love to someone? There are many descriptions of how "men" and "women" are two sexes that may feel the same things but still cannot meet in a common understanding of what love is. In a Scandinavian context the writer Amalie Skram, known for her depictions of married life in the 1880s, explored the incompatibility in how men and women view love. More recently, 1992 brought the all-time best-seller in self-help literature: *Men are from Mars, Women are from Venus* by relationship expert John Gray, which actually gives good examples of poor communication between the sexes.

The Italian sociologist Francesco Alberoni also saw erotic relationships as a matter of gender differences. As he put it in his 1986 bestseller *L'Erotismo*, man and woman must be seen in the light of "a dramatic, powerful, extreme and mystical difference". Alberoni associates the fashion and lifestyle magazines at the women's end of a typical shop rack the focus of female erotic pleasure on touch, materials, scent and colour. Women rub lotion on their skin and decorate their homes, bodies and surroundings with things that provide seductive sensory input for themselves and others. The woman's "feely, touchy, skin and muscular eroticism" not only imbues her with sensuality. It also makes her wish to remain with the person with whom she is intimate.

According to Alberoni, while the man's interest in the woman wanes right after sex (the man regarding this as "the best and most beautiful moment to part"), the woman would prefer to "inhale the smell of his clothing, his male body [...] and the blending of their smells". She seeks continuity, the author asserts, in matters of attention, arousal and tenderness. Based on the sexual relation, the woman makes a link to wanting to share experiences with her beloved, breathing the same air and living the same life as he does.

The idea that "opposites attract" and are united in love is deeply rooted in tradition. We find it symbolised in many different cultures. Its roots in Western culture include writings by Plato, which is why the next chapter takes us back more than two millennia to the classical text *Symposium* – Plato's seminal work on love. Here, in earnest, we encounter the ideal of coming to know not just the sexes but the entire world through love.

THE CONCEPT OF LOVE IN ANTIQUITY

CAN BEING IN LOVE BRING US CLOSER TO BEING GOOD?

Before we return to opposites let us look at another fundamental Western thought also attributed to Plato: We come to resemble that which we love. Love always reminds us of something we already know, he says, but we are transformed through the fond memory coloured by love. We become similar to what we recollect. And because our soul is immortal and holds a knowledge it can no longer remember, we need help to ascend the precipitous ladder of love. The first rung on "Diotima's ladder" (also dealt with below) is beauty, which we discover with the aid of Eros, and the final rung is truth.

Love brings us home to ourselves and shows us our own part in the truth, because in love we find what we did not know we were missing. As explained earlier, that is what makes love ethically relevant and also makes it a question of happiness – especially if we further reason that we can only truly find ourselves through love, where there is no borderline between the I and the world.

Plato believes that by loving what is good we contemplate the good in order to possess the everlastingly good, gaining a spiritual share in what is good. Inversely, by loving something that has no part in what is good we become spiritually poorer. Love (*eros*) begins with physical beauty, ascends to intellectual beauty, and culminates in the love of the Form of Beauty, ultimately leading to the discovery of the Good, which represents the highest truth and source of all virtues. Admittedly we glimpse the immortal when seeing something supremely beautiful, supremely good or supremely dear in this world, but earthly life will always contain imperfection. Even the most beautiful, the best, the most dearly beloved has a partial quality about it. That is why the beauty of the flesh points towards perfection and ideals of what is beautiful, good and true.

In the words of a wise woman, the priestess Diotima, desire in lovemaking transports humans towards the immortal: "with the eye of the mind, man will be enabled to bring forth, not images of beauty, but realities (for he has hold not of an image but of a reality), and bring forth and nourish true virtue to become the friend of God and be immortal, if mortal man may". The *Symposium* has Diotima quoted by Socrates – who was Plato's teacher and the pivotal figure in all his dialogues. The path to truth lies through birth. Not the birthing of children, but a "birth of the soul", as when humans bring something culturally valuable into the world. Plato finds that the greatest things devised by humankind include wisdom "concerned with the ordering of states and families", and "which is called temperance and justice".

CAN VIRTUE BE LEARNED?

In trying to pursue this thought into modern life, we must imagine the mental receptiveness particular to children. As adults we are rarely swept off our feet, captivated by what is before us, as children often are. They dive right in, immersing themselves, body and soul, in the experience as it unfolds. Their empathy and compassion can even make them cry when they hear someone else crying.

Adults may also copy another person's facial expressions, movements and vocalisations. Usually this other person holds sway over them somehow, as with a new manager or sports coach, or an artist giving a live performance. One person can mimic another's body language, intonation and phraseology so completely that it amounts to total identification. This phenomenon, usually short-lived, reveals how readily humans learn from others.

In fact, Plato points out that new generations learn from those older and wiser through mimicry: Enacted knowledge can only be acquired by way of example. We must learn from the courage, justness, goodness and generosity of others, which is the only path that leads to these virtues. In so doing, we invariably fall in love, just a bit. That is why Socrates himself isn't just any old philosopher: He incarnates the very qualities he seeks to imbue in his students. One can only come to know courage or justice by emulating these concepts in an action one envisions one's mentor will endorse.

Plato perceives love as an identification process, an acquisition of qualities. Despite not specifically referring to such unification with others while subsuming their characteristic qualities as "falling in love", he does refer to the situation as "an experience of beauty". He believes it is divine beauty that awakens love. Physical beauty does this too, but it can also tempt one to immediately lie down with the beloved. As Plato drily observes, this merely produces children and not the highest form of achievement – which requires "men who are creative in their souls."

IN SEVENTH HEAVEN

For Plato, ideas belong not on Earth but among the Heavenly Bodies. To know the true nature of the world, humans must therefore die away from it and their souls must unite with the immortality that cannot be found in earthly life, among transitory people and objects.

We find Plato's perception of the heavenly bodies overly idealised and rather odd, but despite our scepticism it has lived on in the expression "seventh heaven" – the outermost sphere in Plato's cosmology. On the other hand, his idea that we discover a compassionate, humane approach to life by engaging with people who personally convey humanity and kindness in word and deed … this idea lives on, notably in education.

This ethical–didactic interpretation of the art of love is just one of many lasting traces Plato left on Western cultures and societies. Much of Plato's metaphysics lives on in our understanding of sexuality as being closely linked to death. This is certainly evident in the art of the Baroque and Romantic periods, but it is also evident in much modern-day art. Consider the Danish director Lars von Trier's film *Antichrist*. It is hardly a coincidence that the couple's young son takes a deadly tumble out a window while his parents are making love in the room next door. The tragic plot begins with this euphoric Fall and moves on to mutilation and death.

The modern Swedish writer Per Olov Enquist also depicts spiritual ruination and erotic desire as interlinked. In his historical novel *The Visit of the Royal Physician*, the young Danish queen Caroline Mathilde realises the significance of her own body, seeing herself as a Holy Grail that unites passion and death. Any man (besides the King) who conquers her will experience exquisite passion – and death. The plot in the novel (and later film) traces the rise and fall of the historical figure Struensee, physician to King Christian VII of Denmark, who was mentally ill. Struensee and the Queen fell in love. After their affair was discovered he was executed and his dismembered body was displayed in public; the Queen was deported to Germany, and the unstable King was dethroned.

In Plato's own thought the link consists, somewhat paradoxically, in the relationship between immortality and perfection, both of which are found in a supreme human state comparable to death. The self becomes real when it lets go of the physical embodiedness which, as physical beauty, took it one step up Diotima's ladder, towards the Seventh Heaven.

SPHERICAL MAN

I have already mentioned several conclusions on the essence
of love from the *Symposium*. This drinking party's seven
revellers take turns making statements about love in the
form of *Eros*, but as usual in Plato's writings the main voice
is Socrates. Another voice, Alcibiades, who professes to be
Socrates' greatest admirer, is not at the party from the start.
Clearly drunk, he arrives with some friends as things are
winding down. He is interesting because he is "in love" in the
exact way one must be in love to learn. He is so enamoured
he even believes Socrates, by force of his erudition, has a
daimonic quality that makes him almost a demigod.

Initially the dialogue is more down to earth, courtesy of
the comedic playwright Aristophanes, who gets a bad attack
of the hiccups almost at once and must skip his turn. Once
recovered, he gives voice to the popular understanding of
love among common folk, recounting the myth of "the
spherical man" and the origins of love:

Humans were once completely round and had four
hands, four legs and two faces on a spherical body. When
they wanted to move fast, they would twirl their eight limbs
acrobatically in the air, whirling forwards as in a continuous
back-flip. But their great strength and audacity made them
arrogant – as happens so often in the Greek myths – and
they tried to rise up to the Heavens and fight the gods
themselves. As punishment Zeus, father of the Greek
pantheon, decided to cut them in two, bisecting them from
top to bottom, just like you halve a hard-boiled egg. From
that moment, human perfection, wholeness and happiness

were over. That is why humans, when fortunate enough to come across their other half, are overwhelmed by tenderness and love. It tempers our passionate nature, and united with our other half we re-create our original state, when each human being really was a whole.

Throughout the text, Aristophanes plays on the bubbly, rolling, fulfilled feeling of being in love, and on how two people feel complete and completed through love: two halves that make up a symmetrical, seamless whole.

EROS THE DAIMON

As hinted earlier, Plato's contribution to the philosophy of love is not an attempt to cast it as divine. Rather, he seeks to bring it down to earth as a ubiquitous longing whose bodily manifestation is desire.

While it is true that Plato has Aristophanes relate the ancient myth of all-healing love, he does not believe it himself. At the drinking party Socrates is Plato's voice, establishing that love is essentially questing, unable to find calm in meeting another earthly being, as a part or as a whole. Love is, by necessity, incomplete and does not become complete by a person encountering their other, better half. Love is and remains desirous, a lust that fills us with fierce yearning directed at something we cannot possess yet identify with so fervently that we wish to fuse with it into a single entity.

No women were invited to the drinking party, of course, but a woman's voice is heard, albeit indirectly, as we've seen earlier. As the evening unfolds, Socrates reports the priestess Diotima's statements, and her words carry special weight: As a soothsayer she is presumed to have links with the divine and know secrets about the true nature of Eros.

Socrates relates that Diotima once convinced him Eros cannot be the most important deity, as the symposium's first five speakers (including Aristophanes) claim. On the contrary, Eros is what the Greeks called a daimon, a tutelary spirit or demigod, precisely because he himself does not possess the beauty, goodness or wisdom that he epitomises in human longing. He cannot be perfect and simultaneously be the deity for the superlative quest to attain perfection. If someone harbours a desire so strong they will strive to fulfil it no matter what, they do so because they do not have that thing. A longing for something springs from its absence.

Beauty cannot be thought into existence, Plato says. Instead, at the top rung of Diotima's ladder, one must devote oneself to contemplating the most beautiful thing of all: the just state. No human "offspring" – offspring of the human mind, created by people – can be more beautifully conceived than this.

ETHICAL LOVE

In discussing beauty we have moved away from sexual relations between people, towards meetings where people can create harmony and justice by creating states and laws. The rationale is that we do not find ourselves when we love. We find virtue. Not virtue as prudishness and propriety, but virtue as integrity and merit and self-betterment. We get better at understanding and telling about the truth. Better at thinking and acting ethically. We get closer to beauty when we love – provided we direct our desire towards attaining the highest truth, goodness and beauty.

Love and moral philosophy have certainly moved further apart after Plato's day, although Spinoza did reunite them in the seventeenth century by describing the unity achieved between the loving person and the harmony of the Universe. Similarly, although in humbler form, the eighteenth-century Scottish philosopher David Hume defined sympathy, beneficence, clemency and moderation as natural human sentiments and virtues. Some twentieth-century philosophers have also perceived love, attention and ethics as preconditions for each other.

This group includes the British writer and philosopher Iris Murdoch and the French philosopher Simone Weil. Their Danish contemporary K.E. Løgstrup formulated *The Ethical Demand*, published in Danish in 1956. In Løgstrup's thinking, ethics mainly deals with the impact we have on other people's lives, and whether we wield our power to enhance or ruin their future happiness and courage.

But before turning to love in its ethical form – the universal "love thy neighbour" concept – let us reflect on why both married and single life can be problematic, due to our exaggerated expectations to love.

LOVE AND DESTINY

The pursuit of romantic love is fraught with danger for those who think that love, to be great, must be absolute. The expectation of finding "the love of our life" becomes problematic if we assume a single person, our one and only, will be able to fulfil our every longing – despite the many other aspects in life both partners must consider. We have already met one portrayer and critic of romantic love, Karen Blixen, who says we must be able to live our lives together on parallel paths: Standing shoulder by shoulder, partners must use the strength love gives them to engage with the world outside their relationship.

After leaving Africa, looking back on her life Blixen realised she had put the love of her life, the British aristocrat and big-game hunter Denys Finch Hatton, in a position that made him unfree. She was not his destiny, nor was he hers. Being the sole mediator of universal healing is a mission few partners are able or willing to undertake.

The Czech-born French writer Milan Kundera is no less sceptical than Blixen about the concept of destiny that underlies the romantic idea of once-in-a-lifetime love. In particular, Kundera judges modern romantic love based on what he refers to as its "laughter of angels". "Two lovers race through the meadow, holding hands, laughing. Their laughter has nothing to do with jokes or humor, it is the serious laughter of angels expressing their joy of being [...] the enthusiastic laughter of angel-fanatics, who are so convinced of their world's significance that they are ready to hang anyone not sharing their joy."

In the glossy perfection of this scene, the laughter of "angel-fanatics" goes beyond the joke and is at once superficial and too solemn, virtually insisting on its own triumph.

Kundera's own romantic novel, *The Unbearable Lightness of Being*, is an attempt to show the gravity in how the female protagonist, Tereza, approaches life, and the upsides and downsides of her approach. Tereza falls in love with Tomas, and she stays in love with him because of her "desire to fall". She wants Tomas, a talented surgeon, to help raise her up to a higher intellectual level. She also wants to keep disgusting things like bodily functions at a distance, attempting to remain physically upright and intellectually elevated by force of her relationship with him.

Tereza's mother, we learn, was raised to see herself as a beauty and feels life has let her down. Now aging, the mother reacts by flaunting her bodily functions and deriding her former beauty and youth. Tereza sees this as shameless, and it scares her. She likens it to the dehumanisation of crowding bodies together.

She finds that Tomas is able to drag her soul to the surface of her body, releasing in her an appetite for life: "All her eagerness for life hung by a thread: Tomas' voice. For it was Tomas' voice that had once coaxed forth her timorous soul from its hiding place in her bowels". Nevertheless, throughout the novel Tereza's vertigo continues to resurface as an urge to return to her mother.

It is hard to say exactly what binds two people together, as Kundera's two main characters illustrate. Paradoxically, things become very heavy for Tomas in *The Unbearable Lightness of Being* when Tereza makes him her destiny and leaves it up to him alone to carry the burden of love. Tomas is a seducer (as discussed later in connection with

Kierkegaard) and he seeks to know womanhood through the diversity of the great, wide world, constantly finding it in new guises. But although he has many women, he also loves Tereza.

THE NATURE OF EROTICISM

Without necessarily living it out, in practice many of us reject the idea of a "one and only" love. We change partners, sometimes repeatedly, and some choose to have more than one partner at a time. Most people no longer realistically expect to find their "one" or "only" love. Still, we have not abandoned the idea of love as a universal healer. Quite the opposite. Never before have people put so much trust in the ability of emotions – preferably passionate ones – to benefit us and free us from a life of diligent concentration. Personal career management is not easy, and it can stretch from our early school years until retirement. Erotic activities are one way to step out of ourselves for a time, away from the self we apply when planning, performing and being accountable.

Importantly, eroticism often cultivates detail. When we have sex we focus on very specific spots or body parts, not least our most private parts. Thanks to them, we can fuse with another person's body while also feeling our own body in action. Sex can make us feel grateful that we have and are a body. Caresses allow others to focus on certain bits of the package while ignoring others.

Some philosophers have emphasised this as a strong point in pornographic representations that actually depict erotic activities without demeaning anyone involved or simply treating them as objects to be used for selfish satisfaction. In such scenarios, our desire can look at the other's exterior as though that were all there is in the world. Here, for a moment, we can let a touch of our hand be everything we are. Erotic beauty does just that: It conceals to accentuate.

Certainly we can feel overlooked when others focus only on our exterior, uninterested in what we hold inside. Conversely, it can be quite pleasant to receive a compliment on our appearance. Work-wise we may already be confident of our talents, skills and resources, but we're not always aware that others take note of our looks or behaviour as well. As a career woman it can be refreshing to have a friend or colleague unexpectedly notice the shell surrounding the core – though some complements do seem irrelevant or out of place. Indeed, recent revelations in the MeToo campaign serve as a harsh reminder to us all that mutual respect is paramount when entering the intricate labyrinth of erotic interaction.

Leaving the topic of erotic love, let us take a closer look at universal agape love. To do this we must once again venture into the history of philosophy. Not as before to the earliest roots of Christianity, but to a nineteenth-century Danish theologian and philosopher named Søren Kierkegaard and his deliberations on "Christian agape love", before treating our final theme: seduction.

UNIVERSAL LOVE

MAN'S GREATEST ASPIRATION

Søren Kierkegaard approaches love much like the apostle Paul, believing love is unselfish and "does not seek its own". Kierkegaard sees love as greatest when it is unmixed with "partiality", his term for our interest-based love for certain people to whom we are partial, preferring them over others.

Showing universal or "brotherly" love means being able to love every other person as a unique other, independent of one's own life story. Being loved in this way, as "a neighbour", is the greatest fulfilment anyone can imagine. There is nothing quite like unconditional love to make the self in a person grow, as Kierkegaard put it. A loving parent's gaze, discussed earlier, has elements of such self-sacrifice. The child is, quite simply, loved. Not because it can smile, or has learned to ride a bicycle, or has graduated from school. Just … because. Parents see children as hugely successful human beings just the way they are.

Meanwhile, the absence of concrete motivation, coupled with the demand that brotherly love need not be justified, is precisely what makes universal love a constant challenge to our emotions, reasoning and self-control. Obviously this is most challenging when it comes to our less lovable neighbours. Universal love must be something we can extend to everyone, even our enemies, but it must also be love in the sense that it is not forced. It is more a demand on oneself, and fulfilling it calls for great self-insight, which in turn enables us to make room for others.

ACKNOWLEDGING DESIRE

Several critics contest Kierkegaard's almost superhuman requirement that one must not mix naturally occurring love – his partiality – with universal love. Most of us would say it is hard not to let existing sympathies influence the extent to which we readily take an interest in others simply because they are there. Sceptics also question Kierkegaard's rejection of partiality as a fruitful element in universal love.

So is there no benefit in being liked or loved for what we do, on a par with being loved for who we are? Can't being gazed upon and desired also contain an element of acknowledgment? And what about a friend's ability to accept our weaknesses? Kierkegaard is not blind to the affection in "partial", preferential love, but he chooses to stand on the side of brotherly love and offer it as the opposite of relationships (erotic or not) where people reduce or constrain each other. On erotic relations, Kierkegaard makes a valid point in arguing that in erotic love partners can struggle and lock each other into fixed images that have more to do with themselves than with their partner. The French philosopher and writer Jean-Paul Sartre certainly agreed with this point, as evident in a well-known line from his play *No Exit:* "Hell is just – other people". We presumably create our image of "the Other" based just as much on our own ideas as on what the other person actually embodies.

UNCONDITIONAL LOVE

The interpretation given here of Kierkegaard's concept of "Christian love" is taken out of its original theological context. Christianity sees love as unconditional because it flows towards us as a loving gift from God, as revealed in Jesus Christ. But when Christ speaks in the New Testament about love, he refers to texts that came before it, including the Old Testament's commands to "love the Lord thy God with all thine heart, and with all thy soul, and with all thy might" and to "love thy neighbour as thyself". With God in this position it is harder to indulge in idolatry, casting something earthly – say, another person – as divine. Nor is it healthy for one person to demand that another person act as their "God". No human being can play God to another, and anyone's imperfections are soon revealed when measured by the exacting yardstick of religious yearning. The question is whether we must distinguish between divine love – and with it universal love – on the one hand and natural, earthly love between humans on the other. In other words: Must we keep *agape*, the Christian love of our neighbour, separate from *eros*, the erotic force that enables people to emotionally connect with others?

As noted, this distinction is clear-cut in Kierkegaard's thinking. Still, we can easily understand unconditional love when it appears in our own lives, as in our relationships with our children. *Sophie's Choice* by the American novelist William Styron is about a mother forced into an impossible decision when the family arrives at Auschwitz: Which of her two children, son or daughter, should be allowed to live? What makes the story so gripping is the reader's conviction that she loves both her children immensely, incomparably. Loving more than one child is not hard. What is unbearably hard is being forced to say whom one loves most, thereby letting a child go. Parental love has no such exclusivity. We love several people at once, and it is impossible to say which child we love the most, whether there are two or three siblings or more. Parental love is a renewing force that keeps growing and giving of itself the more children there are to share in it.

The main idea in universal love is that we can stretch the special gift that lies in love's liberating power to encompass those around us. This is possible because love, as agape, has an openness towards the Other simply because they are human. This love is evoked by the basic value that lies in each and every person. In acknowledging this basic human dignity and value we can embrace every person with a sort of unconditional love, reminiscent of the love God has for humankind.

This relationship of dignity and respect is unlike our relationships with those we love. There is, however, a commonality in the way we either naturally or consciously refrain from making our love dependent on the Other's behaviour and potential shortcomings. These can be painfully evident, but as long as we love our neighbour, showing brotherly kindness and forgiveness, the Other amounts to more than their actions here and now. The reason we can forgive another person for letting us down, even if they seriously fail us, is that shortcomings are not perceived as being on a par with love. We may feel let down if we find someone lying to us or manipulating us, but often, if our love is generous enough, it can tolerate even a severe breach of trust.

Similarly, in lasting, unconditional love as it flows through a relationship with a partner, we can experience life-long erotic attraction to another person. As the passing of time changes their sex appeal and brings on wrinkles or thinning hair, cellulite or a paunch, our partner can retain their allure year after year. This lasting erotic appeal has to do with our partner's whole way of being in the world: the way they grip the steering wheel, the way they treat other people. We are chronically smitten with our partner's actions and attitudes and have come to love them as an expression of who they are. Unlike the swelling, pounding erotic passion of falling in love, this enduring erotic attraction can last for decades.

THE PERILOUS ART OF SEDUCTION

THE TRUSTING SPACE

Symmetry and balance between two people arise when love and emotions are supplemented by a profound and reciprocal trust. Mutual trust also means interdependency, but despite feeling committed one can still experience great freedom in a relationship. Trust creates an extraordinary space where freedom and passion can thrive side by side. Knowing that people count on you and believe in you gives you the strength to be and act in the world. It's not so much our own passionate feelings that enable us to surrender unconditionally to love. It's more the response to these feelings. What we respond to with openness is the other person's receptive openness.

Seduction is the opposite: a critically unbalanced relationship. One person can be wholly at the mercy of another's response when seduced, with the seducer – not the seduced – controlling the manipulation. A person who is seduced into their first experience of falling in love and discovering their sex and sexuality becomes torn. The deceptive element in seduction can be harsh. Surrendering to its passion means becoming dependent on the seducer. The seducer, in turn, comes to possess something we may be gravely unhappy at having given away if, once seduced, we discover the seducer feels no love but is set to move on before the relationship is over.

Sartre describes seduction in *Being and Nothingness,* his philosophical *grand œuvre*, as something between voluntary and forced participation. He claims the seductee is well aware of what's going on, even while pretending the seducer carries full responsibility.

Love as seduction shows with preeminent clarity that identity is not a solid, absolute construct. We can play with our identity and allow others to lead us, only half unwillingly, into alien territory.

DIARY OF A SEDUCER

Nonetheless we can still fall prey, wholly and utterly, to the power of seduction. This is especially ruinous if the process is devoid of love, as in Kierkegaard's *Diary of a Seducer*. He wrote this short novel in Berlin after inexplicably breaking off his long-sought engagement to Regine Olsen (the love of his life) in 1841. His fictitious protagonist, Johannes, is a seducer who unhurriedly but effectively reels in his young prey: the 17-year-old Cordelia. It is fair to say that he, being rather older than she, uses her for sport in his aesthetic game. His ploys to win her affection are nothing if not loveless and callous as he guides her towards the tipping point, the very act of love, then casts her aside, leaving her bewildered and inconsolable.

Earlier we met another fictional seducer: Tomas from *The Unbearable Lightness of Being*. Milan Kundera clearly knows his Kierkegaard and Hegel, as seen in his distinction between the "lyrical" seducer, who is poetic and soulful, and the "epic" seducer, who sees seduction as a factual, objective exercise. A lyrical seducer is a compulsive womaniser seeking in his victims his own ideal of womanhood.

The lyrical seducer never finds the woman in his life, and so he goes on looking. The epic seducer does not seduce fewer women, but he is inquisitive and targeted in his efforts without being a dreamer. He explores the world of women because he is fascinated by the multitude of different ways a girl can cross the threshold into womanhood. As for staging the event, he largely handles that part of the job himself.

Like Tomas, Johannes is a seducer of the epic breed. He plies his trade to find out what sort of finished masterpieces he can create, angling in the endless seas of the female sex only to throw back, throw adrift, each woman who becomes his catch and his creation. Once completed, the work itself is uninteresting. What captivates the seducer is the process. Also, in Kierkegaard's tale Johannes is smitten with himself. That is what makes the author say his seduction is "demonic", meaning it revolves around the self, around itself, its self, in a way that is unfree.

Johannes, self-centred and selfish, clearly exhibits these traits. He wants to possess the world but is not genuinely interested in it. Unlike two other well-known archetypes, Don Juan and Faust, he does not covet or desire the person he seduces. What he enjoys is the gamesmanship, the ruses by which he exposes Cordelia, staging a relationship where every action is aimed to make her think and feel the way he wants her to.

He creates her moods, her dreams, her destiny. He writes letters that lead her to think him better than he really is. He masterminds her longing, fuelling her disgust with the convention of engagement during clandestine embraces at his uncle's house. He makes her detest waiting. He also creates her sexual awareness by gradually shifting her role from listener to talker, moving her to reveal her feelings to him. He creates her passion and her despair, then abandons her to grief. Johannes the seducer poetically invents reality – including the internal reality that is Cordelia-the-woman in the body of Cordelia-the-girl.

THE ART OF LIVING WELL

This brief tale of seduction is actually the first of three parts in Kierkegaard's work about ethical choices entitled *Either/ Or*. On this issue, let us revisit Løgstrup, whom we met earlier. In his philosophy, there is never a vacuum of power in any space or relation between people. As human beings we always have some measure of power to build up or break down the other person's trust in life itself. Either we nurture the things we hold power over, or we treat them with indifference and they wither and die.

Diary of a Seducer shows the problematic aspects of seduction when it becomes a game, a constructed aesthetic diversion for someone bored with life and the world. The problem lies neither in the passion nor in the erotic thrill of seduction. It lies in the destructive force by which one person can create a reality for another and do so as a purely aesthetic exercise, unbound by what they create or shape – in this case Cordelia. Johannes's seductive sport springs from boredom and restlessness, which are unproblematic so long as they do not adversely affect others – as they do Cordelia. Just as the artist leaves the material once it is a fully formed work of art, so the seducer or seductress leaves their sexually created being afloat in their wake.

Transferring a purely aesthetic approach to real life is not without consequences. Unlike the indifferent materials an artist uses, a person's emotions are deeply involved. When a girl steps into womanhood and offers herself to someone she believes returns her feelings, she cannot help but care. In this dynamic, Cordelia-the-woman is powerless because her transition to womanhood calls for someone to respond, yet that person is merely seeking to stage his own performance. He is interested only in himself, wanting to see womanhood displayed for his own gratification, without truly reciprocating her feelings

Some might contend that such staging happens all the time, and that seduction is often precisely what releases a person to the point of accepting the significance and effects of their own sexuality. Certainly, if those involved expect little more than a quick erotic encounter, no problematic imbalance will arise.

FREE LOVE

When two people decide to have an open relationship by giving their love freer rein than usual, they are less concerned than most with what is often called fidelity, allowing more room for erotic playfulness and seduction. Free love therefore assumes that both parties agree to accept involvement with others, seducing and being seduced outside their principal partnership. Here, seduction can be one element facilitating successful erotic interaction with several people. Still, if we are to learn anything valuable from Kierkegaard, then we must insist that seduction be seasoned with a dash of love. Benevolent erotic seduction can make a person grow a little with each new encounter, although there is always the additional element of erotic consumption. If those involved accept the seduction, especially if they expressly opt in rather than relying on an assumed tacit agreement, then victimisation and exploitation become a moot point. That said, all roses have thorns, and we are responsible for our rose – which includes listening when it puts up its defences.

Erotic relations, even in open relationships, often have an element of exclusivity on one side or the other. The fact that a person's passion is exclusive does not mean they cannot love one person and simultaneously have impassioned sexual relations with another. Those living out the premise of free love do still love. However, they insist that the exclusivity – that passionate will and willingness to achieve erotic unity with one particular person – must not affect their loving relationship to the extent of owning the other person's being and all of their time. Anyone who claims ownership over their partner is really keeping them in an iron grip.

If, on the other hand, passion means not owning the other but simply directing all one's attention towards the other, being passionately present in the here and now, then certainly a person is able to cultivate multiple erotic relationships simultaneously. Some people in polyamorous relationships even make structured arrangements so no one feels misled or left out. Be that as it may, even those who voluntarily enter into such relationships can find it hard to hold jealousy at bay, although its severity is alleviated by the openness surrounding the pre-agreed multiplicity.

TWO KINDS OF LOVE

EROS AND AGAPE

Love can be expressed in many ways and encompasses a broad range of experiences. We gain a sense of its vast scope when comparing brief erotic encounters with the deep and long-lasting bonds between parents and children. Each form of love highlights different aspects of human connection and affection In fact, our frameworks for understanding these different types of love have very different roots in two classical concepts I have already mentioned: eros and agape.

Eros is desirous love. In Plato's thinking the word designates the essence of love; in Kierkegaard's work it is "partiality". Plato linked desirous love with something broader than natural, bodily pleasure, which the ancient Greeks called *erga afrodites*, sexual relations. They did not regard such bodily enjoyment as sinful or wicked at all, as later ages did. Knowing oneself also meant being able to show moderation, even when partaking in the pleasures of the bottle, the bed and the table. This culture understood pleasure in its sexual form as an activity that was exhilarating and effervescent, creating foam – *afros* in Greek, hence the image of Aphrodite as the goddess born from the foaming waves.

Plato understands eroticism as awareness of and attention to external beauty that can lead to insight. In ancient Greece, such beauty was primarily found in young men. Fundamentally, however, it is not just our natural surroundings that we as humans must understand with the aid of love. Love also shows us the way to understand human beings themselves. And this is precisely Plato's most decisive contribution to the history of ideas: He expanded the concept of *eros* beyond regular bodily desire to encompass the search for truth. In his view, eros is the divine way of getting to know that part of oneself which is linked to the truth: the soul.

This one kind of love, *eros*, deals with love as the gift people can give each other, completely free of charge. In the biblical understanding, love as a gift is a type of grace whose nature is divine. The other kind of love, beginning with the original Jewish understanding of love – which in the original Greek version of the New Testament texts was called *agape*, translated into Latin as *caritas* – is the all-encompassing love a person can show their sister or brother, their neighbour, even their enemy, and which is modelled on God's love for humankind.

These two tracks in the philosophical history of love merged in the Romantic era, where agape inspired the idea of the self-sacrificing pledge of troth while eros supplied the concept of a passionate link to beauty. Romantic thinking sought to have both these aspects expressed and fulfilled in a love-based relationship. Modern ideas of that one-and-only true love are rooted in this Romantic ideal of what love is, or what we hope it can be.

POOR OLD LOVE

These days our expectations to love are so great that love often seems overburdened. This is rooted in the Romantic blending of the two very different types of life expectations we associate with love. There is the passionate, earth-moving, out-of-body experience of falling and being in love. Then there is the gift of living in a trusting, life-long, warts-and-all relationship with another person we know intimately and love expansively. Both these life expectations are reasonable and even attainable for most people. But love becomes problematic if we want it all, all at once, and if we think that all things great and small in life can be embodied in a single person: our partner in love.

If we are only able to give ourselves lovingly to a person we also find sexually attractive, then our dedication becomes reserved to a very limited circle of people and operates within a sphere that is unwholesomely small. It is good for love to be lived out, exercised if you will, in many different ways – in our relations with our children and other people, yes, but also in a broader sense in the way we relate with love and dedication to our natural surroundings, to the work of a certain author, to a favourite sport or hobby, or to our job.

Being open to finding happiness in relationships like these is actually a way to relieve romantic love of some of our great expectations that it can and should and will ensure our happiness. The answer to whether we live in a romantic era depends on whether the majority of us believe in one-and-only-style true love. Perhaps many of us are, in fact, able to find joy in the fleeting moments of delight and passion, spiritual and physical union, trust and intimacy that come our way amidst the myriad things that make up our daily lives. Nevertheless, based on the inordinate amount of attention given to romantic love, the thought springs readily to mind that perhaps we are putting an unreasonable burden on romantic love in terms of bringing happiness into our lives. And that's really not the best way to treat it – this enigmatic, all-embracing, powerful force we call love.